Locomotives of the London and North Eastern Railway

Written by Alan Bloom
Compiled by David Williams

The Railways Act of 1921 prescribed that the many private railways in Great Britain should be amalgamated into four main groups which became the Southern Railway, Great Western Railway, London Midland & Scottish Railway, and London & North Eastern Railway.

The L.N.E.R. was formed on 1 January 1923 by merger of the Great Central, Great Northern, Great Eastern, North Eastern, North British and Great North of Scotland Railways. The North Eastern, which was the largest of these railways, had already absorbed the Hull & Barnsley Railway in 1922, and the Midland & Great Northern Joint Railway was subsequently absorbed by the L.N.E.R. in 1936.

At amalgamation the L.N.E.R. became the second largest railway in the country and its principal services were from London (Marylebone) to Leicester, Nottingham, Sheffield and Manchester; from London (King's Cross) to York, Newcastle, Edinburgh and Aberdeen, and from London (Liverpool Street) to Cambridge, Ipswich and Norwich. It inherited from the Great Eastern the most intensive suburban service in the world and from the North Eastern and Great Central a very heavy coal and mineral traffic. During the L.N.E.R.'s twenty-five years of existence it owned over 10,000 locomotives.

Amalgamation of businesses is always a painful and frustrating process because of the disruption and displacement it inevitably causes to staff, for loyalties and rivalries die hard. Each of the pre-grouping railways had its own Chief Mechanical Engineer responsible for design and construction of all locomotives, carriages and wagons. Because of its responsibility, the C.M.E.'s post was traditionally one of the most prized positions, second only in importance to the General Manager. At amalgamation a new C.M.E. had to be appointed for the L.N.E.R. and the Directors' first invitation was to J. G. Robinson who had been C.M.E. of the Great Central since 1900. Robinson was, however, already sixty-five years of age and despite pressure from the Directors he declined the post, because he felt a younger man was needed to deal with the stresses of re-organisation which would take several years to complete. The Directors therefore asked Robinson for a recommendation and he strongly advised the appointment of H. N. Gresley, which the Directors accepted.

Gresley was forty-eight and had been C.M.E. of the Great Northern since 1911. He had served his apprenticeship at Crewe Works of the London & North Western Railway and had obtained his first appointment at the Great Northern Doncaster Works in 1905 after posts on the Lancashire & Yorkshire Railway. With hindsight we can now see that Robinson's advice to appoint Gresley was the wisest and best counsel the L.N.E.R. Directors could possibly receive. Under Gresley's direction L.N.E.R. locomotive design, efficiency and performance became second to none and even after Nationalisation in 1948 and right up until the end of steam traction on British Railways, Gresley's best designs remained unsurpassed despite the introduction of nearly 1,000 B.R. standard locomotives from 1951 onwards.

Gresley believed in producing locomotives capable of handling the greatest loads and timing the fastest trains that the Traffic Department were likely to require in the foreseeable future. He disliked the wasteful practice of double-heading as used on

Left: While passenger locomotive development was rapid,
and superseded engines were
quickly discarded, freight locomotives ran for much longer.
Most pre-grouping railways
possessed 0–6–0 tender locomotives, and the Great Northern
was no exception. The H. A.
Ivatt-designed 0–6–0 of 1911
(L.N.E.R. class J6) was the final
development, multiplied to a
total of 110 engines, and serving on G.N. lines intact as a
class until 1955. Here is No.
64232 at its birthplace, Doncaster, on 24 July 1960. The
class was rendered extinct in
1962. (*D. C. Williams*)

Left: Gresley 0–6–0 side tanks
of the L.N.E.R. J50 class were
nominally introduced in 1922,
just before the Great Northern
lost its separate identity and
became part of the L.N.E.R. In
fact early examples were rebuilt
from the G.N. J51 class of 1913.
In total, 102 of these engines
were built new or rebuilt between 1922 and 1937, and
were to be seen in goods yards
in G.N. territory from London to
Leeds, No. 68971 is seen at
Doncaster Works in 1962,
where several could be found as
works shunters. (*Allan Preston*)

Left: The Great Northern Ivatt
saddle tanks introduced in
1897, L.N.E.R. class J52, were
popular machines, and over 100
were built for shunting and trip
freights; most survived into B.R.
ownership. When withdrawn in
1959, B.R. No. 68846 was
restored to original livery as
G.N.R. No. 1247, having been
bought by Captain W. G. Smith.
The locomotive was based at
Hatfield, Haworth and Tyseley
before arriving on the North
Yorkshire Moors Railway,
where the engine surprised
everyone by prodigious haulage
feats on the 1 in 49 from
Grosmont to Goathland. Here
seen at Tyseley on 28 September 1969. (*Dave Cooke*)

Right: It is difficult to imagine that at one time North Eastern Railway expresses were in the hands of such primitive machines as the Fletcher E6. 2–4–0s of 1872–82. No. 910 was among the last to be withdrawn and sent to the original York Museum after renovation. The original livery now carried is very ornate and worthy of study. Though not steamable, No. 910 was removed from the National Railway Museum to take part in the Shildon Rail 150 celebrations, and is here seen in the parade on 31 August 1975. *(D. C. Williams)*

Right: The North Eastern Railway made its money out of goods and mineral traffic, and to do this built and operated a sturdy fleet of 0–6–0 and 0–8–0 tender engines. The ultimate development of the N.E.R. 0–6–0 was the NE class P3, (L.N.E.R. J27) of 1906; 115 of these Worsdell engines were built, early examples having slide valves, and later engines piston valves. B.R. No. 65894, last of the class, and among the last to be in traffic at Sunderland, was rescued by the North Eastern Locomotive Preservation Group for North Yorkshire Moors Railway service. Here seen at Shildon on 31 August 1975. *(D. C. Williams)*

Right: The fifteen North Eastern Railway Raven three-cylinder 0–8–0s, L.N.E.R. class Q7, were usually to be seen on Tyne Dock to Consett mineral traffic, but by 1963 could be spared, safe in the knowledge that 01 2–8–0s and B.R. 9F 2–10–0s could handle the work. Here, on 28 September, No. 63460 stands in South Shields station with a R.C.T.S.–S.L.S. tour train. The locomotive, built at Darlington in 1919, is in the National Collection, and now based on the North Yorkshire Moors Railway. *(John Warr)*

the L.M.S. whenever a train weight or timing requirement was greater than average and he also believed in designing locomotives for specific routes or purposes even if this meant a small number of locomotives in a class. In other words, he believed in 'horses for courses' rather than the minumum number of standard general-purpose designs, although he did believe in standardisation of parts wherever practicable to all classes.

Gresley was also a staunch believer in providing locomotives, large and small, with three cylinders rather than two because of the better starting and acceleration, less coal consumption and less wear and tear to locomotives and track. Apart from additional construction costs, the third cylinder normally had the disadvantage that

it required a third set of valve gear, but Gresley overcame this with a conjugated gear whereby the cylinder between the frames derived its valve motion from the valve spindles of the two outside cylinders. Although much has been said and written in recent years to denigrate the Gresley conjugated gear, the fact is that it has stood the test of time and many of the records for steam traction have been achieved by locomotives fitted with this valve gear.

While C.M.E. of the Great Northern, Gresley had built locomotives which were to have a long life in L.N.E.R. service and these foreshadowed the greater designs which were to come. A two-cylinder 2–6–0 (Class K1) of 1912 was followed in 1913 by a 2–8–0 (Class O1) heavy freight locomotive. The use of a leading pony truck and outside Walschaerts valve gear were both unusual at this early date. The K1 2–6–0 was soon modified with a larger boiler and the well-known Class K2 thus produced. These engines were never very popular in England because they were rough to ride on but they achieved fame on the beautiful West Highland line between Glasgow, Fort William and Mallaig, where they were used singly or in pairs with great success. Painted in L.N.E.R. apple-green, fitted with bigger cabs as a protection against the West Highland weather and given appropriate Scottish names, they were very much at home pounding away up the steep gradients and round the sharp curves. From the K2 Gresley advanced to the K3 and on its first appearance in 1920 the pioneer K3 No. 1000 caused quite a stir. Apart from an experimental three-cylinder 2–8–0, the K3 was the start of the long line of L.N.E.R. three-cylinder

locomotives with conjugated valve gear. The boiler was 6 ft in diameter – the largest that had so far been used. Built for working fast freight and excursion trains, they were very successful and showed their full capabilities during the 1921 coal strike when the train service frequency was reduced and the remaining trains made up to enormous loads of up to twenty coaches. In normal service they were capable of 75 m.p.h. However, within a few years they were overshadowed by later designs and relegated to secondary duties, but a large number were built and the last one was not withdrawn until the end of 1962.

Meanwhile, Gresley had produced the N2 0–6–2 tank engines for the King's Cross suburban services and these were so successful that they worked the major

Left: Ex-Great North of Scotland (D40) Pickersgill 4–4–0 'Gordon Highlander' (B.R. 62277) at Leith Central on 19 April 1965. (*David Idle*)

Below left: Great Central-designed 'Director' D11 4–4–0 No. 6397 (B.R. 62690) 'The Lady of the Lake' at Haymarket shed on 15th September 1935. (*W. A. Camwell*)

Right: Great Central J11 0–6–0 No. 64354 at Mickleover, Derby, on 14 October 1962. Over one hundred were built from 1901. (*Derek Smith*)

Below: North British Railway Reid class J88 0–6–0 dock tank No. 68335 shunts coal wagons at Maryhill, Glasgow in 1962. (*John Warr*)

Left: The Great Eastern J15 0–6–0s were a familiar sight all over East Anglia from their introduction in 1883 until the last was withdrawn in 1962. This T. W. Worsdell class numbered 289 examples in the 1920s, and over fifty survived into B.R. ownership in 1948. Happily, one was saved, B.R. No. 65462. It was restored to G.E.R. wartime grey livery and operated on the North Norfolk Railway. It was photographed at Weybourne, present terminus of the three-mile line from Sheringham on 28 August 1978. (*Derek Tuck*)

Left: The J67 0–6–0 tanks were J. Holden-designed Great Eastern engines dating from 1890. In 1902, later examples with the L.N.E.R. classification J69 were introduced, and these embodied higher pressure boilers, larger fireboxes and water tanks. No. 68601 of this type gravitated from Great Eastern territory, as did several others of the class, and is here shown at Colwick shed, Nottingham on 7 September 1958. (*John Tarrant*)

Left: The Great Northern Gresley mixed traffic 2–6–0s of class K2 first appeared in 1912. Seventy-five were built, and earned the nickname 'Rag-timers' through the affinity of their rough-riding to the dance rhythm of the time. In B.R. days, several were fitted with side window cabs after complaints in Scottish West Highland service. Colwick shed, Nottingham was a popular home for these moguls, and No. 61771 is seen there on 7 September 1958. The last survivors disappeared in 1962. (*John Tarrant*)

Right: A further pointer to the way ahead lay in the Gresley 02 three-cylinder 2–8–0 of 1918, sixty-seven of which were built. The locomotives proved useful for mineral traffic and survived as a class well into B.R. days. The early application of Gresley's conjugated valve gear proved in this case to be less suitable for slow freight work, and the two-cylinder 2–8–0s of Great Central design became the L.N.E.R. standard. No. 63978 at Doncaster shed on 24 July 1960. (*D. C. Williams*)

Below: Development of the K2 came with the 1920 Gresley K3 three-cylinder 2–6–0s, 193-strong. Also rough riding, these 2–6–0s, with 6 ft diameter boilers, were nicknamed 'Jazzers'. Until the introduction of the G.N. Pacifics, they handled expresses out of King's Cross, but they became better known on fast goods services, such as Grimsby fish traffic. Here is immaculate No. 61888 at Colwick. (*John Tarrant*)

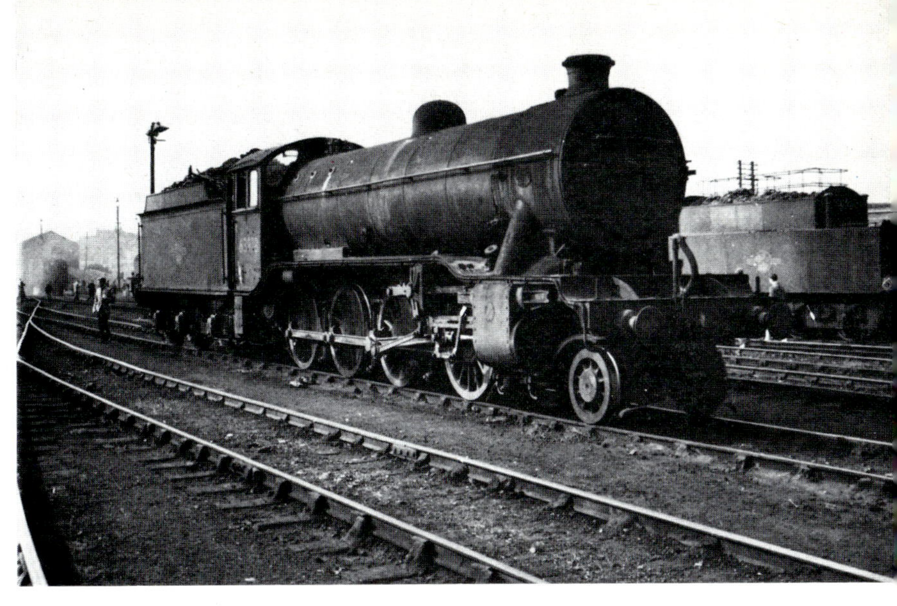

share of this traffic until diesels took over in 1959. A start was also made in fitting the large Ivatt Atlantics (Class C1) with large superheaters. This completely revitalised what were already very good passenger engines to the extent that it would not be an exaggeration to describe them as one of the 'all time greats'. They reached their peak during the 1930s, working the fairly light but fast Pullman trains, but phenomenal performances for their size have been recorded with Atlantics hauling very heavy trains when they have been called upon in emergency to deputise for larger locomotives which had failed.

From this short summary the reader will realise how fast locomotive development on the G.N.R. was proceeding, despite the intervention of the First World War. We come now to the great step forward: the first Gresley Pacific, No. 1470 *Great*

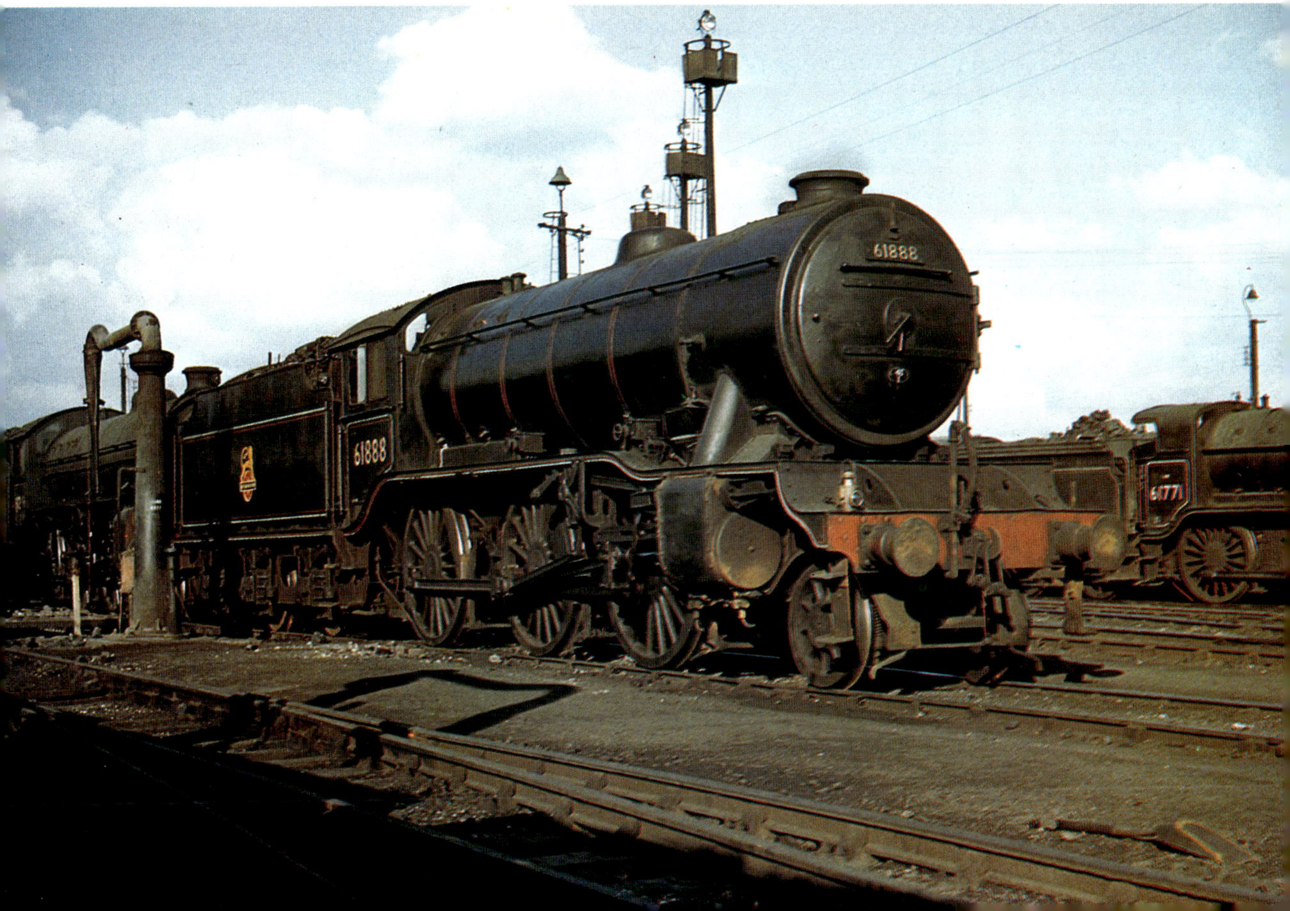

Northern (Class A1 4–6–2). There was a need for more powerful locomotives than the Atlantics to handle the increasing loads of the express trains between King's Cross and the North. Most designers would have gone for a 4–6–0 but Gresley took several steps forward and produced a three-cylinder Pacific with the largest boiler so far built in this country. This boiler was derived from American practice and although several modifications were subsequently found desirable to perfect this first Gresley Pacific design, they were superb locomotives in their original form and could run 600-ton trains on the level at 70 m.p.h. So pleased were the G.N.R. with the first two Pacifics that an order was placed for ten more in 1922 but they were not completed until the L.N.E.R. took over. The first of these ten Pacifics was No. 1472 *Flying Scotsman*, now probably the most famous locomotive ever to run on British rails.

The other constituents of the L.N.E.R. left a mixed bag of locomotives to their new owners. The G.C.R. engines were reliable and well maintained but not particularly sprightly or efficient. The one exception was the Robinson 2–8–0 freight locomotive, which was a robust and simple design and very economical in operation. They were built in considerable numbers for Army service abroad during the First World War and again a number went overseas during the Second World War. The return of those from abroad after 1918 meant that the L.N.E.R. had very little need for any future heavy mineral design.

Below: The 4–4–2 'Atlantics' of the Great Northern Railway were responsible for the increased speed and power of East Coast expresses in the early twentieth century. The first example, with narrow firebox, was class C2 No. 990 'Henry Oakley', built at Doncaster to the design of Ivatt in 1898, and retired to the National Railway Museum at York, where it is seen in August 1975. Both this engine and wide firebox No. 251 are in the National Collection and 'Henry Oakley' has steamed on the Worth Valley Railway. (*Gavin Morrison*)

The G.E.R. power requirements for East Anglia were not exceptional and the N7 0–6–2 tank locomotives, 'Claud Hamilton' 4–4–0s and B12 inside-cylinder 4–6–0s were all adequate for the Liverpool Street suburban and main line services for several years to come. The G.E.R. also possessed a useful stud of 0–6–0 freight locomotives (Classes J15, J17, J19 and J20), many of which lasted until the early 1960s.

The N.E.R. was primarily a coal and mineral railway and in order to handle this traffic they had built sound 0–6–0s and 0–8–0s which continued to work in the North East until the end of steam. Passenger traffic centred around the East Coast Main Line and through trains between London, Newcastle and Edinburgh. The N.E.R. owned the major section of this route from just north of Doncaster to north of Berwick and relied on Atlantic 4–4–2s and 4–6–0s. However, like the G.N.R. they had foreseen the need for a large locomotive for this route and produced a Pacific at the end of 1922 which was little more than an elongated Atlantic.

The North British owned the difficult main lines from just north of Berwick to Aberdeen and from Edinburgh to Carlise. They also owned Scotland's busiest internal passenger line between Edinburgh and Glasgow. For these routes nothing larger than Atlantics and 4–4–0s were available, but for the beautiful West Highland line to Mallaig they had the sturdy and good-steaming 'Glen' class of 4–4–0s.

The Great North of Scotland Railway was very small and amounted to no more than the route from Aberdeen to Elgin and surrounding branches. For this work

they used a very handsome series of small 4–4–0s.

One of the first actions of the L.N.E.R. Directors was to decide upon future locomotive liveries, and Great Northern apple-green with black frames was decided for passenger engines, with black for suburban, goods and shunting engines. It was also necessary to carry out a complete renumbering scheme to avoid duplication.

To meet the immediate secondary power needs of the L.N.E.R., Gresley perpetuated as a stop gap the best of the pre-Grouping designs, until he could draw up his own designs. A batch of G.C.R. 4–6–2 tank locomotives (Class A5) was built for the North East local services and for Scotland, where the most desperate need for improvement existed, a batch of G.C.R. Director 4–4–0s (Class D11) was ordered from private builders. Gresley, however, foresaw that the most important need was to accelerate and improve the main line express service and he devoted his major effort to development of the Pacific.

Comparative trials were carried out in the summer of 1923 between the N.E. and G.N. Pacifics, and the G.N. design proved vastly superior. Thereafter the N.E. engines, despite expense in rebuilding, proved unsatisfactory in service and they were prematurely scrapped in 1936/37. Following upon these trials, forty Pacifics to the G.N. design were ordered with minor modifications to fit them for the L.N.E.R. loading gauge which was tighter than that of the G.N.

At the British Empire Exhibition at Wembley in 1924 L.N.E.R. Pacific No. 4472 *Flying Scotsman* in special exhibition finish was exhibited alongside G.W.R. 4–6–0 No. 4073 *Caerphilly Castle*. Although the Pacific was the larger of the two, the

Left: For Great Eastern suburban trams from London's Liverpool Street station, 134 N7 0–6–2 tanks were built. Originally designed by A. J. Hill, with Belpaire fireboxes, later locomotives were built with Gresley boilers and round-topped fireboxes. Nearly all engines were eventually converted. Withdrawal commenced in 1958, and this is one of the last sad lines of N7s at Stratford shed in 1962. (*D. C. Williams*)

Right: The 'most famous of them all' — No. 4472 *Flying Scotsman* passes through Oxford with the 'Farnborough Flyer' in September 1964. Third of the Gresley Pacifics, and first to appear in L.N.E.R. ownership, No. 4472 worked East Coast expresses from 1923 until B.R. withdrawal in 1963. Seventy-eight other Gresley non-steamlined Pacifics shared these duties (Classes A1 – later A10 – and A3), but No. 4472 became famous because its name was used (officially) five years later for the King's Cross to Edinburgh non-stop train. *Flying Scotsman* visited the U.S.A. in 1970–3. (*Derek Tuck*)

Right: Many variations were to be found of the Great Central Railway Robinson 2–8–0s, L.N.E.R. class 04. Some were sold to the G.W. and L.M.S., and others remained in use in Australia until comparatively recently. Nearly 300 04s entered B.R. service, and were the backbone of Eastern Region mineral traffic. Robinson 04 No. 63913 (originally a 5 ft 6 in. diameter boilered engine, but here with a 5 ft 0 in. boiler) alongside a Thompson 01 on Staveley G.C. shed in 1963. (*Allan Preston*)

Left: The 'Claud Hamilton' 4–4–0s, L.N.E.R. class D15, and the Gresley-boilered rebuilds, the 'Super Clauds', class D16, collectively numbered 121 locomotives. When new, these locomotives were used on Great Eastern express services, but in later years worked secondary services in East Anglia. Here is class D16 No. 62545 of King's Lynn ex-works after its last repair at Stratford in 1956. (*Max Lock*)

'Castle' had the largest nominal tractive effort and to test which was the best, trials with an engine from each class were held between King's Cross and Doncaster, and Paddington and Plymouth. Although luck was not on the L.N.E.R. side there is no doubt that the 'Castle' won the day. This caused much consternation to the L.N.E.R. authorities and the Pacifics were quickly modified from the lessons learned from these trials. Thus was born the so-called super Pacific Class A3, which had a 220 lb/in.² boiler pressure compared with 180 lb in the original design, and redesigned valve gear to make the locomotive much freer running. The valve gear of the original engines was also modified quickly and they were eventually all fitted with 220 lb boilers and classed A3, weighing (engine only) 96 tons. The majority were named after winners of the Derby and St Leger and in their modified form became capable of handling with reliability and competence the heaviest and fastest East Coast expresses right up until the introduction of diesels. A number of the older engines ran over two million miles before withdrawal and *Flying Scotsman* was the first locomotive in this country to authentically reach 100 m.p.h., in 1934. A year later No. 2750 *Papyrus* reached 108 m.p.h., which remained the speed record in this country until the advent of the A4 streamlined Pacific.

In 1928 the L.N.E.R. inaugurated the longest non-stop run in the world with the *Flying Scotsman* train between King's Cross and Edinburgh – a distance of 393 miles. To enable enginemen to change over half-way a number of Pacifics were fitted with corridor tenders. These were the largest tenders ever to operate in Great Britain.

By this time a need existed for a more powerful 4–6–0 for the East Anglian services. The Great Eastern had been built on the cheap as befitted a line serving a small population and no heavy industry, and consequently the bridges were not strong enough to take locomotives with heavy axle weights like the Pacifics. A three-cylinder 4–6–0 (Class B17) was therefore designed within the constraints of the route. Known as the 'Sandringhams', these locomotives performed usefully on the express services from 1928 until 1951 when the 'Britannias' took over. A second batch of B17s with larger tenders was built for the Great Central services and these were named after famous football clubs. In some ways the B17s were a

Left: Eighty one of the Great Eastern Railway B12 4–6–0s were built 1911–1928. No. 61572, the last survivor — with round-topped boiler — poses near Sheringham on the North Norfolk Railway on 1 October 1977. (*Graham Mallinson*)

Right: Work-stained North Eastern Railway Raven 0–8–0s Nos. 63363 and 63428 gather round Tyne Dock shed turntable in 1964. L.N.E.R. class Q6, the class were in use from 1913 until 1967. (*John Hollowood*)

Below: 105 N.E.R. 0–6–0s of class P3 (L.N.E.R. J27) were built between 1906 and 1923. No. 65855 climbs towards Silksworth with empties in 1967. (*Tony Bending*)

Left: L.N.E.R. B17 4–6–0 No. 61664 *Liverpool* is seen standing in London's Liverpool Street station in 1959. Seventy-three of these nominally Gresley-designed three-cylinder 4–6–0s were built between 1928 and 1937. (Detail design was the work of the North British Locomotive Company.) Initially the engines were drafted to the Great Eastern line, while later locomotives worked Great Central express services out of Marylebone. These 'Sandringhams' and 'Footballers' (named after stately homes and football teams) could put up good performances on passenger work, but their rough riding and unreliable steaming made them unpopular at certain depots. In 1960 they became extinct, including the rebuilt Thompson boilered B2s and the two former streamlined examples. (*Michael York*)

Left: The Gresley D49 4–4–0s, seventy-six of which were built from 1927 onwards, were of similar ancestry to the B17s, but specifically designed for secondary passenger work in North East England and Scotland. They were named after 'Hunts' and 'Shires', and achieved a moderate degree of success in operation. The last survivor, B.R. No. 62712 *Morayshire* was withdrawn in 1961 and privately preserved in Scotland in L.N.E.R. livery as No. 246. It left its present home at Falkirk to take part in the Shildon exhibition in 1975. (*D. C. Williams*)

Left: In B.R. days as No. 60700, the lone Gresley W1 4–6–4 heads an express out of King's Cross for Peterborough. Originally built in 1929 as a four-cylinder water tube boilered 4–6–4, the engine was unsuccessful and rebuilt with three-cylinders in 1937 and streamlined in the already successful A4 mode. The engine's large firebox and hungry appetite never endeared it to enginemen and the 1959 scrapping came as no surprise.

Right: Six of these three-cylinder P2 2–8–2s were built in 1934–6 by Gresley for Edinburgh–Aberdeen services. They were fine machines but unsuitable for the sharp curvature in Scotland. The locomotives were rebuilt by Thompson in 1943–4 (see page 26). No. 2002 *Earl Marischal* was caught appropriately at Aberdeen Ferryhill depot on 26 May 1936. (*R. J. Buckley*)

Right: The North Eastern Raven B16 three-cylinder 4–6–0s, originally seventy in number and built in 1919–24, were successful but unspectacular locomotives, and were used principally in the York, Hull and Leeds areas on a wide variety of mixed traffic work. Twenty-four locomotives were rebuilt, seven of these from 1937 onwards with Gresley's two Walschaerts gears and derived motion for the inside cylinder, and seventeen locomotives from 1944 onwards to Thompson's specification with three independent Walschaerts gears. One of the last survivors was No. 61438, a Gresley rebuilt engine, here seen passing Swithland sidings with an L.C.G.B. railtour from London Marylebone to Nottingham Victoria on 14 October 1962. (*Derek Smith*)

Right: Gresley J38 0–6–0 No. 65914 was photographed at Kinneil Colliery, Fife, on 11 April 1966. Thirty-five of these locomotives were built in 1926 for use in Scotland, being a small-wheeled adaptation of the Gresley J39 0–6–0, 289 of which were built between 1926 and 1941. Unlike the larger type which disappeared in the very early 1960s, the J38s survived longer, No. 65914 being the last to receive a heavy workshop repair, and was withdrawn in 1966. The class could be seen almost universally on mineral traffic over the former North British system. Not surprisingly, the locomotives were found to be inferior in steaming and riding to the N.B.R. 0–6–0 of classes J35 and J37. (*David Idle*)

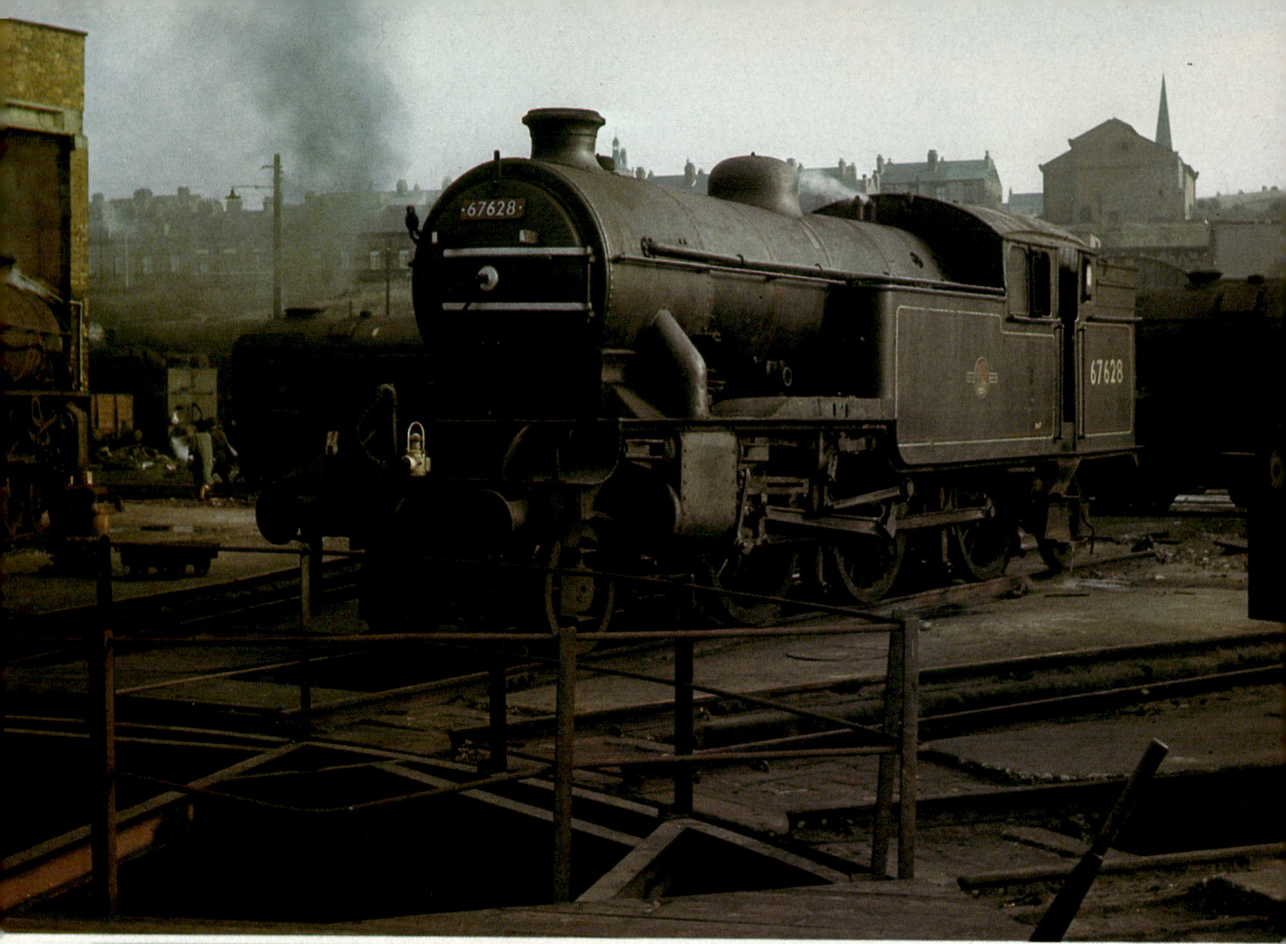
67628
67628

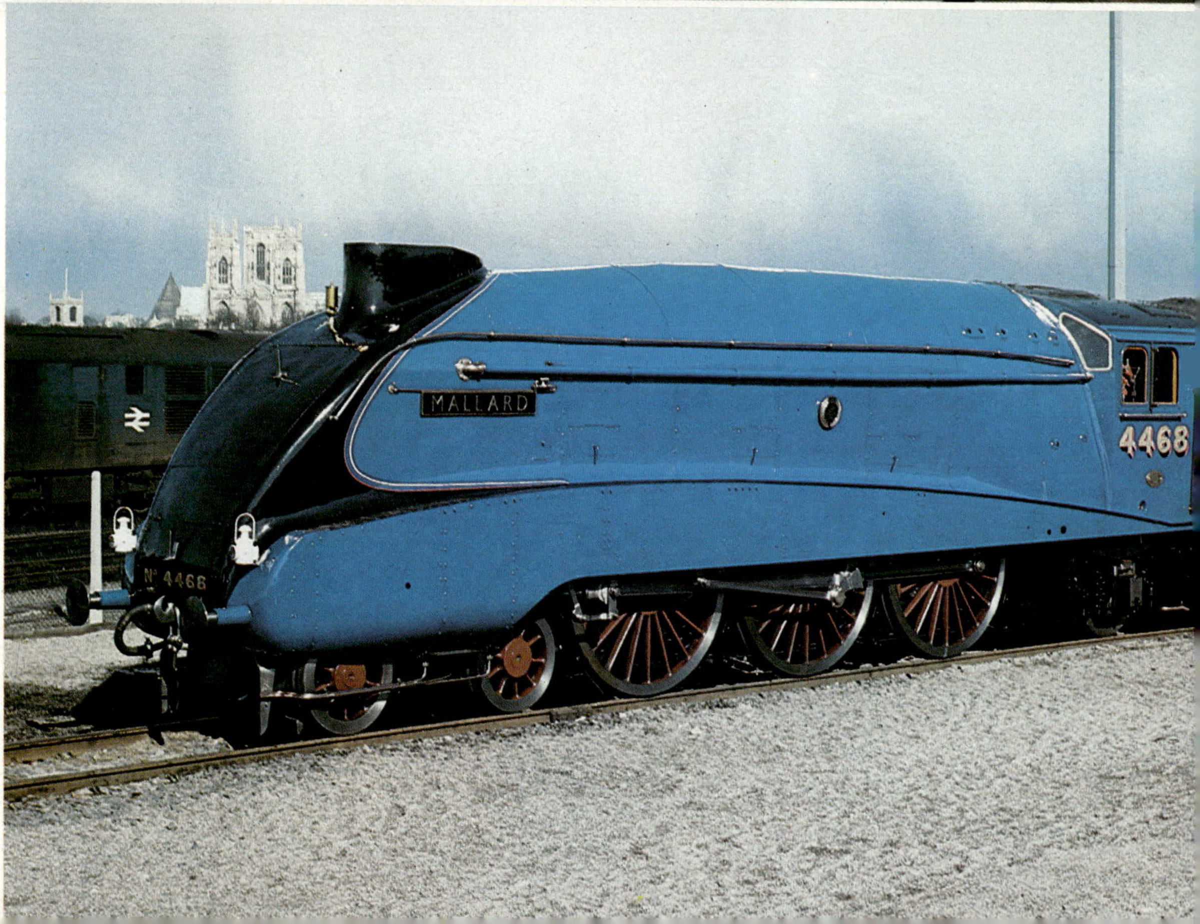
MALLARD
4468

disappointment, for they showed little advance in power over the G.E.R. B12 4–6–0s, but the physical conditions of the routes prevented a larger locomotive which Gresley would certainly have preferred.

The North East and Scotland had a number of important secondary routes, like Leeds to Scarborough and Edinburgh to Perth, which required an intermediate passenger locomotive somewhat better than the pre-grouping designs. A three-cylinder 4–4–0 (Class D49) was therefore produced in 1927, but although perpetuated to a fairly large class of seventy-six locomotives they were never very popular on fast trains because of their rough riding.

Besides being forward-looking in designing locomotives to cope satisfactorily with traffic and competition of the foreseeable future, Gresley was equally keen on improving efficiency and testing alternatives to development of the conventional design first introduced by George Stephenson. Consequently he drew up plans and built in 1929 a massive 4–6–4 compound with four cylinders and a marine-type water tube boiler pressed at 450 lb/in.² instead of the conventional fire tube boiler at 200 lb/in² pressure. Early promise was not proved in subsequent service and No. 10000 proved troublesome and expensive to maintain. Its design developed intense interest and there can be no denying the ingenious work involved. In 1937 it was rebuilt as a conventional three-cylinder 4–6–4 and streamlined. In this form it proved more satisfactory, particularly with heavy trains.

The Edinburgh to Aberdeen route had always been a difficult line to operate. Gradients were steep, curvature sharp and most of the important stations were located in dips. Moreover, the most important trains, like the 'Aberdonian' sleeping car express, were loaded to over 500 tons which was beyond the capacity of a single Pacific. As the Pacifics were too heavy to be piloted, double-heading with two smaller engines was necessary and Gresley met this challenge with the giant and magnificent P2 Class 2–8–2s. He had already produced a 2–8–2 (Class P1) freight engine in 1925 to test the operation of 100-wagon coal trains between Peterborough and London, and the P1s proved capable of hauling successfully loads of up to 1,600 tons. The P2s, however, represented a considerable advance forward. Initially, two were built in 1934 and they were the first locomotives to be built by the L.N.E.R. since 1930, the economic recession of that period having caused a policy of refurbishing older locomotives. The first locomotive, No. 2001 *Cock o' the North*, was the largest and heaviest passenger locomotive built up to that time in this country, the engine weighing 110 tons without tender. It was also the most powerful, for apart from eight coupled wheels it had a very large boiler with a fire grate of fifty square feet. With three 21 in. diameter cylinders exhausting to double blastpipes it was as impressive in appearance as it sounded and performed. As an experiment, No. 2001 was fitted with poppet valves and the second engine, No. 2002 *Earl Marischal*, fitted with the conventional Walschaerts/Gresley conjugated valve gear. Gresley had been a strong advocate of the setting up of a Locomotive Testing Station in Great Britain but progress had lapsed during the economic depression. He therefore sent No. 2001 to France for testing on the Vitry plant and out on the line. The results achieved on these tests were very good and 2,800 horse power was recorded at the drawbar; the highest ever recorded for a British locomotive. The poppet valves, however, did not prove as satisfactory in service as the conventional valve gear, and 2001 was converted to conventional form and along with 2002 given a normal streamlined wedge-shaped front end. A further four locomotives were built, Nos. 2003–2006, and the six locomotives proved themselves complete masters of the Edinburgh–Aberdeen route.

As the older designs from the pre-Grouping companies became due for new boilers or other heavy repairs, the opportunity was taken to rebuild them as more efficient locomotives. The G.E. 'Claud Hamiltons' and B12 4–6–0s were among those to receive this treatment. Another very successful conversion was the N.E.

Below Left: Gresley's three-cylinder V2 2–6–2s were often referred to as the 'engines that won the war'. The prototype No. 4771 *Green Arrow* was introduced on a fast goods of that name in 1936, running from King's Cross to the North. It was soon found that these 6 ft 2 in. engines were as effective on express passenger as freight. Their work on the Aberdeen fish trains and Waverley route freights will be particularly remembered. No. 4771 is shown roaring through Culgaith with a railtour train on the ex-L.M.S. Carlisle–Leeds main line on 27 March 1978. (*Bob Green*)

Right: In B.R. days, the V2s were numbered 60800–60984. Some engines did good work on the erstwhile Great Central main line, and long after their transfer away, York engines still worked onto the Great Central. Here, No. 60961 raises the echoes approaching Rugby Central with a Dringhouses–Woodford 'fitted' on 24 October 1964. (*Derek Smith*)

Left: 'Sir Nigel Gresley' was one of the most famous A4s, running over many living-room carpets in the 1940s and '50s. No. 4498 is here seen on a Tyseley–Didcot special at Harbury near Leamington on 1 July 1973. Built at Doncaster in 1937, the locomotive worked East Coast expresses and latterly Glasgow–Aberdeen trains until B.R. withdrawal in 1966. It was repaired at Crewe Works in 1967, and has been seen all over Britain. Unlike 'Mallard' it is preserved in post-war condition without valances. (*D. C. Williams*)

Right: London and Edinburgh A4s were well maintained, and most possessed corridor tenders for working 393 miles non-stop. The Gateshead engines, however, were generally more humdrum, working similar turns to other Pacifics on the Newcastle strength. Here No. 60001 *Sir Ronald Matthews* (not the prototype of the class) heads through Benton with the 16.30 Newcastle–Berwick semi-fast on 28 August 1964. (*David Idle*)

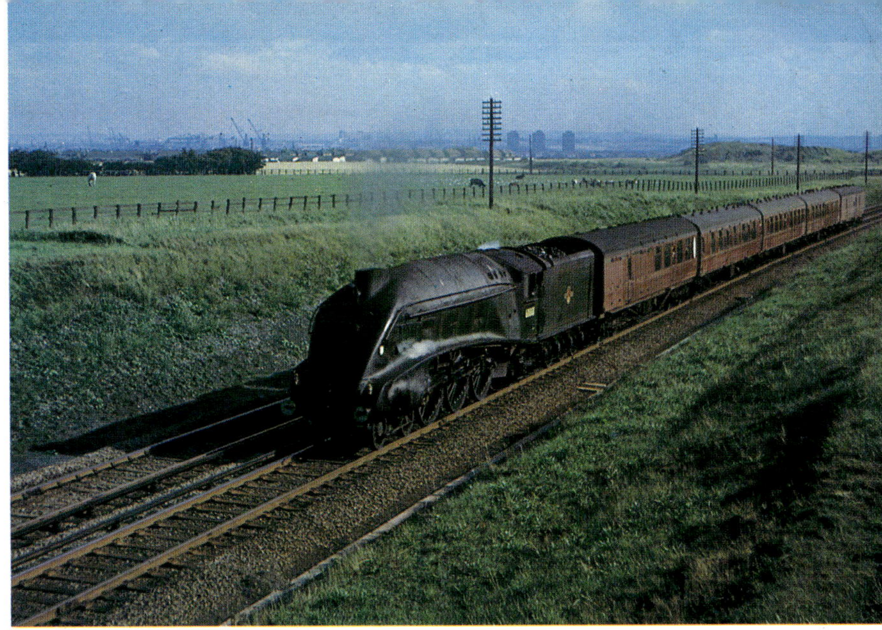

B16 4–6–0 which was rebuilt with conventional Walschaerts/Gresley valve gear for the three cylinders instead of the original three separate sets of Stephenson's valve gear. In its rebuilt form, the B16 was an excellent locomotive for working fast freight and excursion trains.

Other locomotives produced in the late 1920s and early 1930s included the J38 and J39 0–6–0 freight locomotives. These classes were identical except that the J38 had smaller driving wheels for service in Scotland. A 2–6–2 tank locomotive with three cylinders (Class V1) was also built in large numbers for important short distance semi-fast passenger services. The largest locomotive ever to operate on a British railway was also built during this period, namely the unique Garratt 2–8–0+8–2 provided for banking coal trains on the Worsborough incline. It

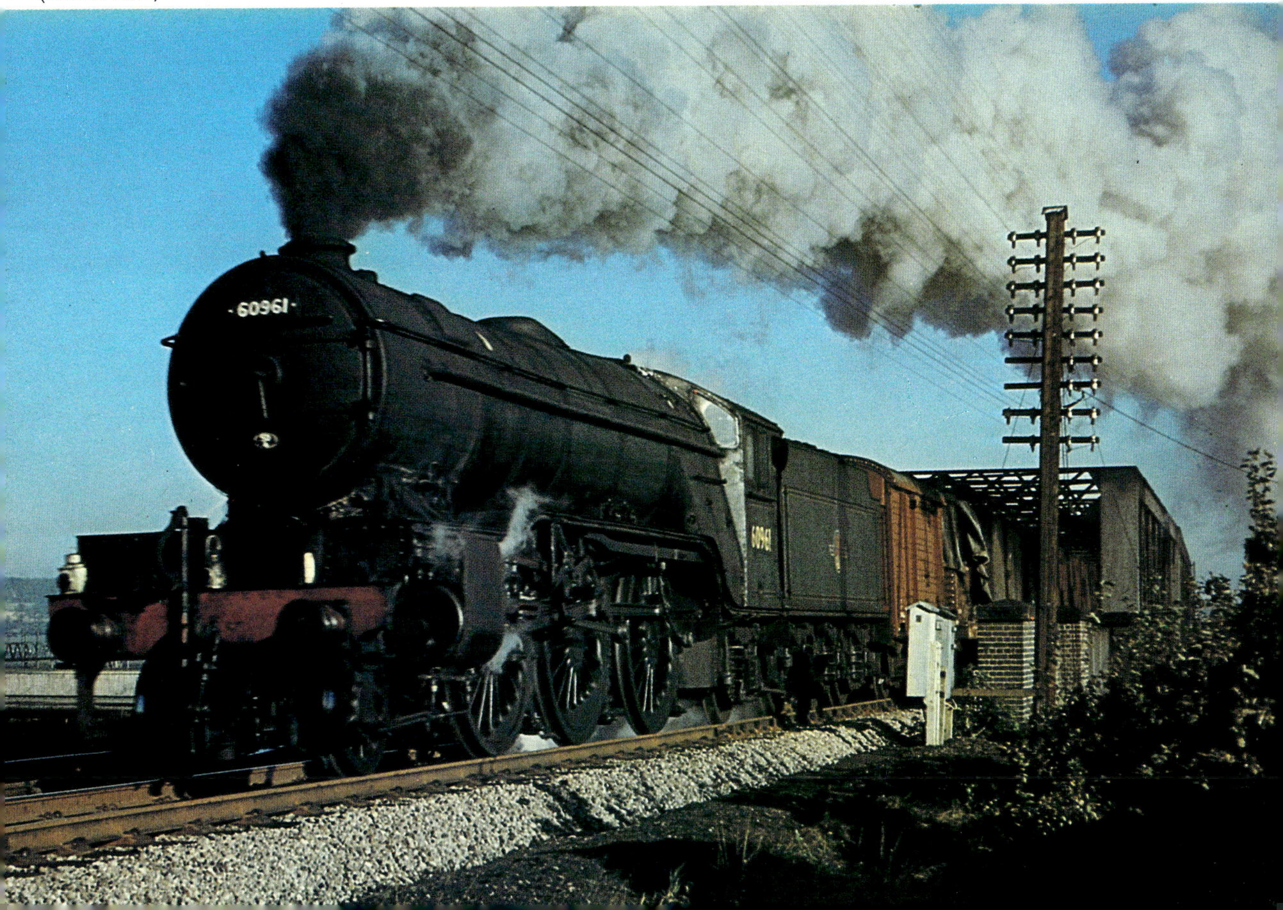

Left: Six of the Gresley three-cylinder K4 2–6–0s were built at Darlington in 1937–8 for service on the Glasgow–Fort William (West Highland) line. The K2s were becoming over-taxed and the K3s were too heavy for this line; hence the K4s, with a smaller boiler mounted on K3-type machinery. No. 3442 'The Great Marquess' was the second of the class, and after withdrawal from Thornton Jcn. (Fife) in 1961, as No. 61994, was bought by Lord Garnock and restored to L.N.E.R. livery. Used on railtours over B.R. it reached the Severn Valley Railway in 1972. Photographed at Darlington North Road on 3 October 1964. (*David Idle*)

could do the work of two 2–8–0s.

We come now to the final and greatest period of L.N.E.R. locomotive development. As the country rose out of the economic depression, so did the desire to improve express passenger and freight services. Competition from the car and lorry was also becoming much keener and a serious factor to be reckoned with. The A1 and A3 Pacifics were performing very satisfactorily and were the equal or better than anything on the main lines of the other three main line companies. Trials were held with these locomotives between King's Cross and Leeds in 1934 and King's Cross and Newcastle in 1935 to ascertain their capabilities for achieving a four-hour timing over the 268 miles between King's Cross and Newcastle. This was to prove that they could at least be the equal of a suggested German diesel railcar which would not be able to offer the same standard of comfort as an improved ordinary train. Although the A3 could have satisfactorily managed the four-hour timing in normal service, Gresley decided improvements should be made and the famous A4 Pacifics were conceived. The most visible external change was the streamlined casing which was of great publicity value and very effective in lifting smoke clear of the driver's view ahead. Internally the improvements over the A3 produced perhaps the most outstanding express passenger locomotive ever to run in this country. No. 4468 *Mallard* achieved the world speed record for steam traction in 1938 of 126 m.p.h. – a record which still stands. The class as a whole, which numbered only thirty-five engines, achieved more recorded speeds of 100 m.p.h. or over than all the rest of the express locomotives in this country put together. In heavy-load haulage they have produced horse-power in excess of 2,500 and they raised the standard of performance on the East Coast Main Line during the late 1930s to the best in Great Britain. Their hardest working was the 'Coronation' train which, between King's Cross and York, was timed at an average speed of 71·9 m.p.h. and was between 1937 and 1939 the fastest train in the British Empire.

For fast freight work Gresley designed his last large locomotive. This was the Class V2 2–6–2, often known as the 'Green Arrow' after the prototype loco of the class, first put to use on a fast freight service of the same name. This wheel arrangement had not been used in this country before for tender locomotives but Gresley seized the advantage it offered over the 4–6–0 to provide within the loading gauge a large wide firebox. It was thus a pocket Pacific and for most purposes its equal. Into the V2 Gresley put all the worthwhile design improvements he had used over his long career as a C.M.E. The result was a locomotive of outstanding flexibility and versatility which was equally at home on heavy express passenger work as on fast or slow freight trains, and no other railway had such a useful engine with which to enter the Second World War. As mixed traffic engines they continued to be built during the war and finally totalled 184 locomotives. They became known as 'the engines that won the war' because of their prodigious feats of haulage and the terrible punishment they were subjected to in keeping traffic moving.

Following upon the speeding up of the East Coast services with the introduction of the 'Silver Jubilee', 'Coronation' and 'West Riding Limited' streamlined trains, attention was then given to the Liverpool Street to Norwich services.

Unfortunately, weight restrictions prevented any larger locomotive than the 'Sandringham' Class B17 4–6–0 which had first appeared in 1928, but two of the most recent locomotives were fitted with A4-style streamlined casings for working an accelerated 'East Anglian' express. This train was also provided with new carriages, having interiors comparable with the streamlined trains.

The increasing demand for seats on services between King's Cross, Leeds and Newcastle resulted in designs being drawn up in the late 1930s for a super A4 Pacific with a higher boiler pressure for the light-weight 'flyers' and a mammoth 4–8–2 for the heavy load express. Unfortunately, the Second World War stopped both these projects.

Greater demand for sleeping and dining cars on the West Highland line had led to more double-heading of the Class K2 2–6–0s which were limited to 220 tons when working singly. Six new locomotives of the 2–6–0 wheel arrangement were therefore built in 1937/39 specially for this line (Class K4). With their three cylinders and higher boiler pressure they were able to haul 300 tons unaided over this difficult route.

Traditionally, secondary routes had to make do with 'pensioned' main line locomotives. This made good economic sense but by the end of the 1930s the large number of pre-grouping locomotives were coming to the end of their economic life and were not suitable for speeding up the secondary services in the same way as the Pacifics and V2s were doing on the main lines. Gresley therefore produced the V4

2–6–2, although the incidence of the war resulted in the first locomotive not being finished until 1941. Named *Bantam Cock*, it had the usual three cylinders, and with a wide firebox and high pressure boiler it incorporated all the best design features which had gone into the A4 Pacifics and V2s. The second locomotive had a steel firebox and was the first locomotive in this country to be fitted with a thermic syphon in the firebox. These two locomotives were veritable 'Rolls-Royces' and quickly proved themselves in service. Unfortunately, Gresley died on 5 April 1941 and his successor as C.M.E., Edward Thompson, had other ideas. It is a great pity that the war and Gresley's death meant the cancellation of the order for more V4s as there seems little doubt that, had peace continued and with good maintenance, the V4 would have revolutionised secondary services and provided an excellent 'stand-in' locomotive for main line emergencies.

Edward Thompson was already sixty years of age when he succeeded Gresley and had been mainly concerned with repair and maintenance of L.N.E.R. locomotives. He preferred to use two cylinders instead of three whenever possible and disliked the conjugated valve gear. One of his first acts was to remove the valancing from the streamlined casings of the A4s, B17s and W1 to make the motion more accessible; this was a sensible step in the difficult war years when there was a shortage of maintenance staff.

Thompson's first design was his best and only real success. This was the B1 4–6–0 of which 410 were eventually built. This was a simple two-cylinder locomotive and the L.N.E.R. answer to the L.M.S. 'Black Five'. It was also Thompson's alternative to the Gresley V4 2–6–2 and, in the wartime austerity circumstances then prevailing was probably a better solution. It quickly established itself as a sound general-purpose locomotive of medium power and was widely used throughout the system.

The six magnificent P2 2–8–2s built for the Edinburgh to Aberdeen route were proving difficult to maintain in the grim early wartime years and Thompson took the drastic action of converting them to Pacifics in 1943/44. As such they provided a proving ground for his own design of Pacific, the first of which appeared in 1946. In the rebuilt engines (Class A2/2) the conjugated valve gear was discarded in favour of three separate sets of Walschaerts valve gear and the drive divided so that the outside cylinders drove the centre coupled wheels and the inside cylinder the leading coupled wheels. This produced a most ungainly appearance. When sent back to Scotland after rebuilding, the A2/2s proved most unpopular due to their lower adhesion and they were soon sent back to England where they were latterly based at the secondary main line depots of York and Peterborough. They were the first L.N.E.R. Pacifics to be scrapped in 1959/61. Thompson received severe criticism for this rebuilding and many experts were only too ready to point out what excellent locomotives the P2s would have been for handling the very heavy wartime loads south of Edinburgh where the less severe line curvature would have had less effect on the long coupled wheelbase.

Thompson next built four Pacifics in place of the last V2 2–6–2s. These became

Right: A B1 in B.R. livery; No. 61076 surmounts the 1 in 41 of Cowlairs Incline with a Glasgow Queen Street–Fife train on 11 August 1960. (*Gavin Morrison*)

Below: Fifteen Thompson 6 ft 2 in. Pacifics of class A2/3 were built in 1946–7; they were not very well liked, suffering from poor adhesion and frame fractures. Here is No. 60520 *Owen Tudor* at Gateshead shed on 28 October 1962. These three-cylinder engines were kept away from the top express work, though three lasted in Scotland until 1965. The prototype was appropriately named 'Edward Thompson' (B.R. No. 60500). (*David Idle*)

Class A2/1 and were virtually V2s with the rebuilt P2 cylinder arrangement. This again produced a most ungainly locomotive and all four locomotives had been scrapped by 1961, indicating how inferior they were to the V2.

In 1945 one of the most controversial rebuildings in the whole of locomotive history occurred. Thompson had already displayed his intense dislike for the work of his predecessor by dispersing Gresley's senior staff to other duties, rebuilding the P2s and discarding the conjugated gear. His action in 1945 of taking the original *Great Northern* Pacific of 1922, No. 1470, and rebuilding it to his own design (Class A1/1) as a prototype for a new express passenger locomotive was taking his feelings to the extreme, particularly as he refused to listen to arguments that another Pacific should be used for the rebuilding. By any normal standards No. 1470 would have ranked highly for preservation as a milestone in the development of the steam locomotive. As it was, the rebuilt No. 1470, although reasonably successful, was inferior to the A3 and A4 Pacifics and was condemned in 1962.

The fifteen Thompson standard Pacifics of Class A2/3 which were derived from the rebuilt P2s and A2/1s appeared in 1946/1947. They suffered the same faults and unpopularity as their predecessors and although the class was not finally extinct until 1965 they did very little work in their last years.

Thompson's other rebuilds included two-cylinder versions of the B17, D49, K3 and K4. From a performance point of view none of these were any improvement over the originals. He also produced the L1 2–6–4 tank for outer suburban services but these quickly became run down after overhaul due to the diameter of the driving wheels relative to their stroke and their tendency to slip.

Left: The final development of the Robinson 01 2–8–0 was to be found in the Thompson 01 class. Fifty-eight 04s were built with new cylinders, Walschaerts valve gear, B1-type boilers, raised running plates and side window cabs from 1944 onwards. Classified 01, these engines were thus virtually new machines. They were to be found mostly in the southern area of the L.N.E.R., particularly on Annesley–Woodford Halse freights. No. 63773 is shown. (*Allan Preston*)

Right: One hundred Thompson L1 2–6–4 tanks were constructed between 1946 and 1950, four actually appearing before nationalisation. They were tried on London suburban services, but suffered from lack of adhesion and extremely bad riding. At Marylebone, they were found decidedly inferior to G.W.R. 2–6–2Ts and L.M.S.R./B.R. 2–6–4Ts, and most were eventually banished to the countryside. The northernmost stud were on Teeside; here No. 67766 heads the 19.50 Whitby–Middlesbrough at Ruswarp on 24 July 1958. (*Michael Mensing*)

Right: Sanity returned to L.N.E.R. Pacific design with the 6 ft 2 in. Peppercorn A2s of 1947–8. Fifteen were constructed, of which No. 60532 *Blue Peter* is preserved. Only the first, No. 525 *A. H. Peppercorn*, appeared in L.N.E.R. livery. Immaculate No. 60527 *Sun Chariot* heads the *West Coast Postal* 15.30 Aberdeen–London Euston at Larbert, near Stirling, on 11 April 1963. The Pacific was working to Carstairs: (*David Idle*)

Left: The six Gresley P2 2–8–2s were rebuilt by Thompson as 6 ft 2 in. Pacifics in 1943–44, and magnificence was reduced to mediocrity. The engines steamed poorly, lost their feet easily and were written off early (1959–61). Here, A2/2 No. 60504 'Mons Meg' runs light from New England shed through Peterborough North station on 22nd September 1958. (*Derek Smith*)

Left: Seventy-five Ministry of Supply 0–6–0 saddle tanks were purchased by the L.N.E.R. in 1945, numbered 8006–8080 and classified 'J94'. Gorton, Colwick, York South and Darlington had very strong allocations of these engines, and No. 68050 is shown shunting at Darlington North Road Works on 3 August 1964. These 48-ton locomotives were last used by B.R. on the Cromford and High Peak line. Many are preserved, including a few ex-B.R. examples. (*D. C. Williams*)

Below: Final development of the East Coast Pacifics came with the introduction of the 6 ft 8 in. Peppercorn A1 Pacifics of 1948–9. Forty-nine were built, numbered 60114–60162, and they handled much of the East Coast traffic, particularly London King's Cross—Leeds Central. No. 60138 *Boswell* of York accelerates through Finsbury Park with the 11.15 King's Cross—Leyburn troop train on 2 June 1962. (*David Idle*)

Edward Thompson retired in June 1946 and so ended one of the most controversial periods in British locomotive history. There is no doubt he was C.M.E. during a very difficult period, but apart from the B1 his designs were short-lived and in the Indian summer of steam traction on the ex-L.N.E.R. the Gresley designs, despite their age, remained supreme.

Arthur Peppercorn succeeded Thompson and he quickly set about reinstating Gresley's design staff and restoring many of his design features with the exception of the conjugated valve gear. The order for thirty Thompson A2/3 Pacifics was cut by half and the balance of fifteen redesigned to produce a much more compact and better looking locomotive. These were classified A2 and, after proving satisfactory in service, Peppercorn designed a new standard Pacific on similar lines to the A2 but with larger driving wheels. These became Class A1 and forty-nine were constructed between 1948/49. In the immediate post-war years the new A1s proved themselves

Right: Another York A1 is shown here. No. 60121 *Silurian* rests in the sunshine at York shed on 4 October 1964. By this time, York A1s were finding all-year employment mostly on freight duty, Dringhouses–Tyne Yard being the usual run. Only on summer Saturdays were these speedy and powerful machines to be found on express passenger duty. (*Derek Tuck*)

Right: One of the six Gresley three-cylinder K4s was rebuilt by Thompson in 1945 as a two-cylinder machine. In this form it was successful, and formed the prototype for seventy K1 2–6–0s (planned under Peppercorn's aegis, but actually appearing after nationalisation). Though classified as 'mixed traffic', these engines rapidly became rough riders after overhauls, and were usually seen in freight service. No. 62027 of Consett depot, is seen at Waskerley, Co. Durham during the working of the R.C.T.S. 'North Eastern Tour' on 28 September 1963. (*John Warr*)

Right: A more normal view of a K1 is provided by this shot of No. 62045 attacking the climb northwards from Hartlepool in 1967 with empties for Sunderland. Many of the K1s were to be found in the North East, at York, Darlington, Thornaby, Hartlepool and Blyth depots. (*J. A. Bodfish*)

to be reliable and competent locomotives and the average mileages for the class as a whole between heavy repairs reached 93,000. Five of the A1s were fitted with roller bearings and they ran an average of 118,000 miles between heavy repairs. These are the best figures ever achieved by an express passenger locomotive in this country.

Peppercorn also produced a standard two-cylinder 2–6–0 (Class K1) to replace the large number of ageing 0–6–0 freight locomotives which became expensive on maintenance as speeds increased. Like the B1 4–6–0s, the K1s were used throughout the L.N.E.R.

With Nationalisation on 1 January 1948 the L.N.E.R. ceased to exist as an entity and was split up into the Eastern, North Eastern and part of the Scottish Region of British Railways. Until the new B.R. standard designs could be produced, existing L.N.E.R. locomotives of the A1 and K1 designs continued to be built.

One of the first actions of the new masters was to set up interchange trials between representative express passenger, mixed traffic and freight locomotives of the S.R., G.W.R., L.M.S.R. and L.N.E.R. These trials took place in 1948 and their objective was to decide the best features of existing designs which could be incorporated into the new B.R. standard locomotives. The L.N.E.R. locomotives acquitted themselves well and the A4 Pacific produced the lowest coal and water consumption of all the locomotives.

As the country grew out of the post-war period and competition from road transport increased, the demand for faster passenger and freight trains became vital if the railways were to retain their existing business let alone obtain a larger share of an increasing market. By 1950 the A1s and A2s were still proving their worth but the older Gresley Pacifics were suffering from steaming and mechanical problems due to poor quality coal and inadequate maintenance. When the A4 Pacifics were originally built, four had been fitted with Kylchap double chimneys and one A3 Pacific was similarly experimentally fitted in 1937. These five locomotives had always been very much better performers than their sisters and all the other members of these classes were modified similarly in the late 1950s. The double blastpipes, better maintenance, and a redesigned inside big end completely solved the steaming and mechanical problems and the revitalised A3s and A4s saw steam out in triumph on the East Coast Main Line. Their performances outclassed those of their pre-war years and main line steam performance on the ex-L.N.E.R. became better than anywhere else on British Railways. As the A3s and A4s re-emerged to their former glory, the younger Thompson and Peppercorn Pacifics were relegated to secondary duty and the last of the A4 class outlived the last of the newer designs. As diesels were introduced on main line work the A3s and A4s were sent on to routes over which they had not previously operated and they quickly built up excellent reputations on the Leeds–Carlisle–Glasgow and Aberdeen–Glasgow lines. When finally withdrawn some of the A3s had run over two million miles since new.

Six V2 2–6–2s were also fitted with Kylchap double blastpipes late in their life to improve their capability when substituting for failed diesels. No better final tribute could be paid to L.N.E.R. locomotive design than to compare the performance data of V2 No. 60845, when tested on the Swindon test plant, with the leading designs of the other Grouping Railways and B.R. standard designs. From the following test data it will be seen that, taken overall, the V2 produced the best results despite the fact that the design was virtually unchanged since 1936.

Left: Experiments at Swindon enabled eight V2 2–6–2s to be modernised with the double exhaust arrangement, also outside steampipes to separate cylinder castings in place of the previous 'one piece' arrangement. No. 60862 has arrived at King's Cross with the 07.05 from Peterborough on 25 May 1963. (*David Idle*)

	Lbs/i h.p. hour		Cylinder efficiency %	Boiler efficiency %	Combined boiler and cylinder efficiency %
	Coal	Steam			
Duke of Gloucester (4–6–2)	1·81	12·2	15·7	68	10·7
Britannia (4–6–2)	1·95	13·2	14·0	72	10·1
B.R. Class 5 (4–6–0)	1·96	14·3	13·3	72	9·6
B.R. Class 4 (4–6–0)	2·10	13·7	14·1	68	9·6
Ivatt Class 2 (2–6–0)	1·85	14·4	13·3	77	10·2
B.R. Class 9 (2–10–0)	1·85	13·6	13·7	73	10·2
L.N.E.R. V2 (2–6–2)	1·80	13·2	14·7	75	11·0
L.M.S. 'Duchess' (4–6–2)	2·40	14·2	13·1	62	8·1
L.M.S. Class 5 (4–6–0)	1·83	14·0	13·6	73	9·9
G.W.R. 'King' (4–6–0)	1·6	13·8	14·0	73	10·2
S.R. 'Merchant Navy' (4–6–2)	2·5	16·0	12·0	65	7·8

Back Cover: A last reminder of the backbone of the L.N.E.R., the hard working freight locomotives of the North East. Ex-North Eastern Railway Worsdell Class P3 (L.N.E.R. Class J27) 0–6–0 No. 65811 of Sunderland depot blasts up the branch from Ryhope Grange Junction to Silksworth Colliery. Photographed in the summer of 1967. (*J. A. Bodfish*)

By way of conclusion, a brief outline of where L.N.E.R. locomotives may be found today is given opposite. The L.N.E.R. were pioneers in the setting up of the first railway museum at York (following the Stockton and Darlington Rly centenary celebrations of 1925), and upon these firm foundations was planned the National Railway Museum of today.

Left: 0–6–0 side tanks of North Eastern Railway design (L.N.E.R. class J72) were built in two separate periods; eighty-five were built between 1898 and 1925, and a further twenty-eight engines by British Railways at Darlington in 1949–51. These later engines were indistinguishable from the earlier batch except by running number, and were the last engines constructed to L.N.E.R. constituent design. Thus No. 69023 was only eleven years old when this view was taken at Gateshead on 28 October 1962. 69023 is preserved as *Joem* and has operated on the Worth Valley and Derwent Valley lines in recent times. (*David Idle*)